GROWING UP
BLACK
AND
PROUD

A GUIDE FOR TEENAGERS

PETER BELL
WITH JIM BITNEY

JOHNSON INSTITUTE®

Minneapolis

Growing Up Black and Proud
A Guide for Teenagers

Johnson Institute-QVS, Inc.
7205 Ohms Lane
Minneapolis, MN 55439-2159
612-831-1630

ISBN 1-56246-064-1

Design and Production by MacLean & Tuminelly
Cover Illustration by Felix Ampah
Text Illustrations by Harry Pulver, Jr.

Printed in the United States of America

93 94 95 96 97 / 5 4 3 2 1

The cover artist, Felix Ampah II, was born in Ghana, West Africa. He has an MFA degree, and he teaches in addition to maintaining a full service art studio.

1. Tribal Celebration (West Africa)
2. Proud Teenagers (East Africa)
3. Sharecropper (1898)
4. Civil Rights March (1963)
5. All Black Infantry (American Civil War)
6. Black Family (Models)
7. Rosa Parks
   (Inspired Civil Rights Movement)
8. Mary McLeod Bethune
   (Educator, Civic Leader)
9. Fredrick Douglass
   (Publisher, Abolitionist)
10. Jackie Robinson (Brooklyn Dodgers)
11. Booker T. Washington (Educator)
12. High School Graduation (Models)
13. Entertainer/Singer
14. Teenage Models
15. Politician
16. Professional Basketball Player

Contents

1

IDENTITY

"Learn to see ...
listen ... and think
for yourself."
Malcolm X

"... ask in your
black heart who it is
you are."
Imamu Amiri Baraka

Who are You?

DO YOU KNOW WHO YOU ARE? As a whole package? Really? Let's see. Suppose the package on the next page is you. Suppose someone is interested in the package but wants to know what it really is—really contains. Could you show or identify in pictures or words who you really are? Do you know your ingredients? Could you list them? Give it a shot.

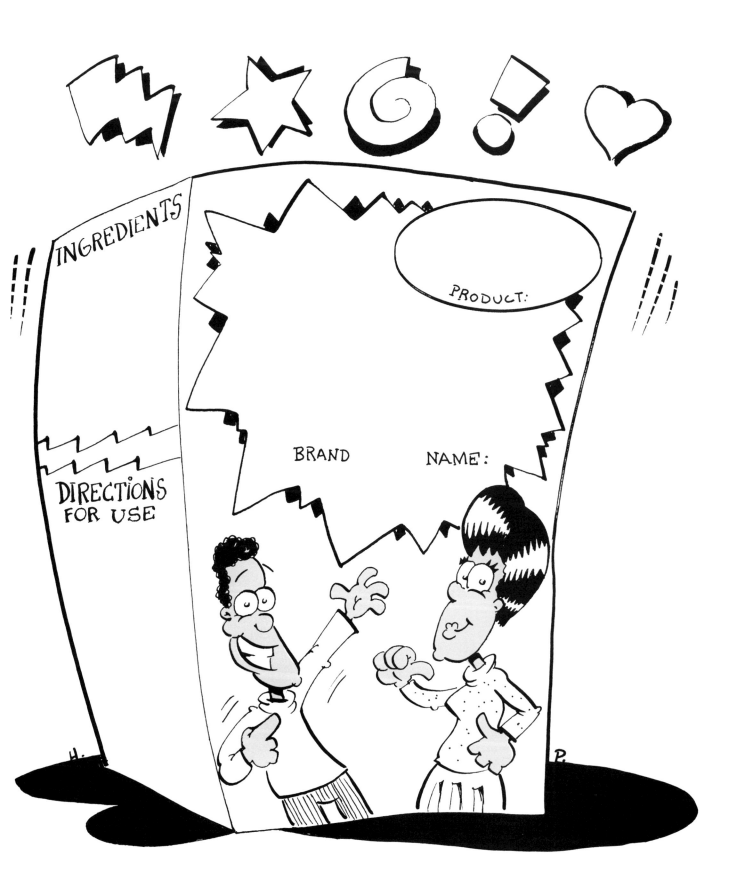

Quality Ingredients

YOU'VE GOT SOME QUALITY INGREDIENTS. Taken all together, these ingredients make up your identity. They say: "This is me. This is who I am." And that's important, because you may think you're just like a whole lot of other kids, but you're not. You and your identity are as unique as your fingerprints. There never was another you, and there never will be.

Right now, your identity might be a sister, a brother, a student, or an athlete. As you grow older, however, your identity will change to wife, husband, parent, teacher, musician, doctor, grandparent, and the like. Your identity may also change depending on where you live. Different parts of your identity may be stronger at one time or another. Every day you're discovering new things about your identity. Every day you're becoming more and more you.

There's an important part of your identity that doesn't get talked about a lot. In fact, you may never mention it or think about it, even though it's always with you, shaping you, identifying you. What we're talking about here is your racial identity.

Maybe you think that racial identity is no big deal or that some folks are just trying to make it into a big deal. Well, maybe it's no big deal for whites. But it probably is for you, a young Black person. Maybe many whites don't seem to have a racial identity, but you do. It comes from your status as a minority in this country. If whites were a minority, then they might have more of a racial identity, too.

For you, racial identity asks the question: "What does it mean to be Black?" It's a big question and a tough one. Many things can shape your racial identity: for example, the way movies and TV portray Blacks; how your family and relatives view and talk about the Black community; how your friends talk about the Black community; and how the schools treat Black history. "What does it mean to be Black?" is a question that all African-American people in this country must answer. It's one you're going to have to answer, and answer for yourself.

As you go on developing other parts of your identity, like your values, goals, and way of behaving, your racial identity goes on developing, too. Don't let it go on without you. If you do, someone else will be telling you what it means to be Black. And you don't want that. Why? Because your identity is the way you see yourself. And the way you see yourself influences the way you make decisions about your life—decisions about career, sex, alcohol and other drugs, and so many other important things. Those choices are yours. Developing a strong and positive racial identity will help you keep them that way.

▶ Name two Black individuals or groups with a strong racial identity.

_____

_____

Name two Black individuals or groups with a weak
▶ racial identity.

_____

_____

Name one white individual or group with a strong
▶ racial identity.

_____

2

HOW ARE BLACKS VIEWED? STEREOTYPING

"We are positively a unique people. Breathtaking people. Anything we do, we do big! Despite attempts to stereotype us, we are crazy, individual, and uncorral-able people."

Leontyne Price

Snap Judgments

HAVE YOU EVER HAD TO MAKE A SNAP JUDGMENT? Have you ever had to think fast and make a quick decision about something or someone? If you have, that's a snap judgment. Now, just in case you've never been in a spot like that before, you're in one now. Why? Because you're about to make some snap judgments right now.

Four people are pictured on this page. Each one is labeled with a letter. Look at each person.

Finished? Good.

Okay, let's make some snap judgments. Quickly answer all eight questions below by circling the letter that you think most African-American kids your age would think corresponds to the picture. But hustle! You've only got 15 seconds. Get busy!

DECIDE . . .

1. Who's the richest?   A B C D

2. Who's the dumbest?   A B C D

3. Who's the toughest?   A B C D

4. Who's the most trustworthy?   A B C D

5. Who's the best athlete?   A B C D

6. Who's in trouble with the police? A B C D

7. Who's the most religious?   A B C D

8. Who's the smartest?   A B C D

Stereotypes Are Not Different Types of Stereos

STEREOTYPING LETS US MAKE QUICK JUDGMENTS about people we don't have time to get to know or don't really want to know. We often act on the basis of these quick decisions. For example, imagine you're a waiter or a waitress. A customer who's dressed really fine comes in. There's a Rolex on his wrist, and he's wearing a designer suit. The man's expensive jewelry and clothes lead you to figure that he's rich (a stereotype!), so you give him better service in the hope of getting a big tip.

Stereotypes aren't just for individuals. Groups of people also have stereotypes about them.

SOME ARE POSITIVE:	**SOME ARE NEGATIVE:**
JEWS ARE HARD-WORKING.	JEWS ARE STINGY AND RICH.
ASIANS ARE SMART.	ASIANS ARE HUMORLESS.
BLONDES HAVE MORE FUN.	BLONDES ARE STUPID.
BLACKS ARE GREAT ATHLETES.	BLACKS ARE LAZY.

Our popular culture often reinforces stereotypes like these through movies, television, and music.

As you can see, there are some really big problems with stereotyping and stereotypes.

1 Stereotypes are based on broad, imperfect—and often wrong—views about a very large group. For instance, there are a lot of Jewish people in the world. Not all of them are hard-working. Not all of them are rich.

2 Stereotypes often prevent people from being judged on the basis of their individual strengths or weaknesses. For example, Michael Jordan is Black. He is a great athlete. But he is definitely not lazy.

3 Stereotypes pressure individuals in a group to live up to the group's positive images or stereotypes. For example, an Asian teen may feel pressure to do well in school due to the stereotype that says, "Asians are smart."

4 Finally, stereotypes may also pressure someone to prove that he or she doesn't fit a group's negative images or stereotypes. For example, the same Asian teen who feels pressured to do well in school might also feel pressured to "be one of the crowd," so no one will think he or she is some weird and mysterious egghead.

We all need to make snap judgments—quick decisions—now and then. There are lots of situations in life that seem to say, "Hey, think fast!" For example, it may be okay—and smart—to stereotype a group of young men and boys who are wearing gang colors "trouble" and to cross the street as they approach. It may also be okay to figure that a white southern male's rude and condescending behavior is due to racism, depending upon the circumstances. The important thing to remember, however, is that *our stereotypes of **whole other groups** are often **wrong**.* Never substitute a stereotype for taking the time to get to know someone.

Blacks on Blacks

HOW DO YOU THINK BLACK PEOPLE LOOK AT other Black people? Do you think Blacks may stereotype one another? Look over the list of items below. For each item, mark on the line how you think the African-American community views itself.

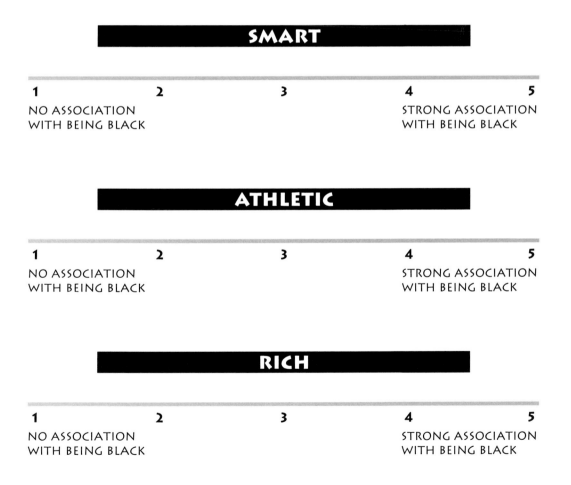

SMART

1	2	3	4	5
NO ASSOCIATION WITH BEING BLACK			STRONG ASSOCIATION WITH BEING BLACK	

ATHLETIC

1	2	3	4	5
NO ASSOCIATION WITH BEING BLACK			STRONG ASSOCIATION WITH BEING BLACK	

RICH

1	2	3	4	5
NO ASSOCIATION WITH BEING BLACK			STRONG ASSOCIATION WITH BEING BLACK	

REPUBLICAN

1	2	3	4	5

NO ASSOCIATION
WITH BEING BLACK

STRONG ASSOCIATION
WITH BEING BLACK

HARD-WORKING

1	2	3	4	5

NO ASSOCIATION
WITH BEING BLACK

STRONG ASSOCIATION
WITH BEING BLACK

GOOD STUDENT

1	2	3	4	5

NO ASSOCIATION
WITH BEING BLACK

STRONG ASSOCIATION
WITH BEING BLACK

WELFARE

1	2	3	4	5

NO ASSOCIATION
WITH BEING BLACK

STRONG ASSOCIATION
WITH BEING BLACK

HONESTY AND TRUSTWORTHINESS

1	2	3	4	5

NO ASSOCIATION
WITH BEING BLACK

STRONG ASSOCIATION
WITH BEING BLACK

DEPENDABLE

1	2	3	4	5

NO ASSOCIATION
WITH BEING BLACK

STRONG ASSOCIATION
WITH BEING BLACK

BAPTIST

1	2	3	4	5

NO ASSOCIATION
WITH BEING BLACK

STRONG ASSOCIATION
WITH BEING BLACK

SINGLE PARENT

1	2	3	4	5

NO ASSOCIATION
WITH BEING BLACK

STRONG ASSOCIATION
WITH BEING BLACK

BUSINESS PROFESSIONAL

1	2	3	4	5

NO ASSOCIATION
WITH BEING BLACK

STRONG ASSOCIATION
WITH BEING BLACK

DEMOCRAT

1	2	3	4	5

NO ASSOCIATION
WITH BEING BLACK

STRONG ASSOCIATION
WITH BEING BLACK

MUSLIM

1	2	3	4	5

NO ASSOCIATION
WITH BEING BLACK

STRONG ASSOCIATION
WITH BEING BLACK

GOOD DANCER

1	2	3	4	5

NO ASSOCIATION
WITH BEING BLACK

STRONG ASSOCIATION
WITH BEING BLACK

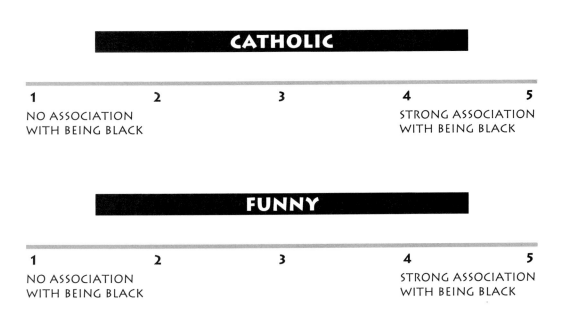

CATHOLIC

1	2	3	4	5
NO ASSOCIATION WITH BEING BLACK			STRONG ASSOCIATION WITH BEING BLACK	

FUNNY

1	2	3	4	5
NO ASSOCIATION WITH BEING BLACK			STRONG ASSOCIATION WITH BEING BLACK	

POOR

1	2	3	4	5
NO ASSOCIATION WITH BEING BLACK			STRONG ASSOCIATION WITH BEING BLACK	

List the three *strongest* associations you feel the Black community has of itself.

1. _____

2. _____

3. _____

List the three *weakest* associations you feel the Black community has of itself.

1. _____

2. _____

3. _____

Whites on Blacks

HOW DO YOU THINK WHITE PEOPLE look at Black people? Do you think whites may stereotype Blacks? Look back over the list of items on pages 17 to 21. For each item, use a red pen or pencil to mark on the line how you think whites view the African-American community.

List the three *strongest* associations you feel whites have of Blacks.

1. _____

2. _____

3. _____

List the three *weakest* associations you feel whites have of Blacks.

1. _____

2. _____

3. _____

3

THE IMPACT OF INTEGRATION

"I hear that melting pot stuff a lot, and all I can say is that we haven't melted."

Jesse Jackson

Out or In or Within

WHEN PEOPLE MOVE TO A NEW LAND, they have to make some hard and painful decisions:

▶ *They could stay separate.* If they choose to do this, they would live only with people from their own group, speak their own language, and keep their own foods, religion, music, and dress.

▶ *They could integrate into the larger society.* If they choose to do this, they would hang onto their roots, keep some of their "old" ways, but also include some of the culture from the new environment—the food, drink, dress, and the like—in their way of living.

▶ *They could assimilate.* If they choose to do this, they would blow off all the old traditions and ways of life. Then they'd take on the traditions and customs of the new country.

Even though many African Americans have lived in the United States for generations, most African Americans today are faced with these same three options. As an African American, you need to decide whether to remain separate, to integrate, or to assimilate into this country's dominant culture.

Separation, integration, and assimilation: each of these options has its good and bad features.

Separation. If you choose to be separated from the broader society, you may have a greater sense of security and belonging. The people around you would be of the same race, dress alike, eat the same sorts of foods, and share similar roots. Living separated may help you feel more connected to your parents and relatives. At the same time, however, you may also feel that you don't quite fit in with other kids. They may not understand or appreciate the music you like, the food you eat, or how you talk and dress. You may view the "things" of the broader society as things to be hated or to be jealous about. You may feel safe within your group, but locked out of the larger group.

Integration. If integration is your choice, you may benefit from knowing and understanding both the Black and the white world. You may be able to function successfully in both. At the same time, however, you may not feel totally accepted in either world. Other African-American friends and family may feel uncomfortable with the white friends you may have. White friends may put pressure on you to give up some of your racial identity—to stop acting or talking or dressing so "Black."

Assimilation. African Americans who choose assimilation into the dominant culture usually have a higher degree of success in the work world. At the same time, however, they often feel disconnected from their own community and are often accused of forgetting where they came from.

Which option should you choose? Well, most of you will need to experiment with what option is right for you. Your choice may be the right one for you today, but not tomorrow. In fact, you may change many times as you grow into adulthood. Now that you know the pros and cons, keep your options open.

Separation, Integration, and Assimilation: A Fine Line

Let's see where you stand on the fine line of separation, integration, and assimilation.

SEPARATION   **INTEGRATION**   **ASSIMILATION**

1. Mark an **X** to show where you see yourself today.

2. Mark an **O** to show where you think you were five years ago.

3. Mark an **I** to show where you think your parents stand.

4. If a brother or sister (or friend) stands far apart from you on the line, show his or her position with a **Z**.

5. Show with a **Y** where you would place most of your Black friends.

6. Show with a **B** where your Black friends would place you on the line.

7. Show with a **W** where your white friends would place you on the line.

The Best for Me, Right Here, Right Now

WRITE WHERE YOU ARE ON THE FINE LINE of separation, integration, and assimilation. Tell why—or why not—you believe it is the best place for you, right here, right now.

_____

_____

_____

_____

_____

_____

_____

_____

_____

_____

_____

_____

_____

_____

4

CULTURAL BOUNDARIES

"Never knowing who he was, always copying everyone else, the monkey one day cut his throat."

Zulu Proverb

Crossing Boundaries

EVERYONE HAS BOUNDARIES. A boundary is a sense of separateness and individuality that prevents people from being too close to us, but also allows for closeness when needed. Boundaries help us to have an identity of our own. Some boundaries allow or prevent physical closeness, like someone standing too close to us. Other boundaries deal with more personal things, for example, someone asking you if your parents fight at home, or whether you've ever been kicked out of school. These kinds of boundaries are called *personal boundaries*. You'll know that a personal boundary's been crossed when someone "gets too close" either with his or her body or with a question or comment. You'll find yourself wanting to say "Get outta my face" or "Mind your own business."

Many African-American teens have specific boundaries that touch on sensitive topics in the Black community, for example: African-American families headed by women, with no father around. We call these *cultural boundaries*. You may feel differently talking about topics like these with your Black friends than with your white friends. Why? Because these topics might reflect stereotypes that make the Black community look bad. You may feel pressured to explain or to justify certain actions or behaviors that are associated with the Black community. In some cases, cultural boundaries will touch on issues of personal shame and guilt.

When someone asks you a sensitive question or raises a touchy subject regarding race, the first question you have to answer for yourself is "What is this person's motivation?"or "Why did he or she ask this question?" If someone asks about Blacks and crime, for example, you'll need to decide whether the person is being racist or insensitive, is stereotyping, is asking a legitimate question, or is just making a comment. Remember that sometimes people ask insensitive questions about the Black community, but they aren't always asked out of meanness. They're asked out of a lack of information.

Once you figure out the person's motivation, you have to figure out how to respond. You can choose from a number of options:

1

Make a joke about it.

4

If you think the person's reason for asking the questions is screwed up, refuse to answer *and* tell the person how the question makes you feel.

2

Don't answer the question. Blow it off or change the subject.

3

Answer the question, but also tell the person that the question is close to being racist or is a stereotype. Give the person the correct information, but also explain that questions like that make you feel uncomfortable, or angry, or upset, or sad, and so on.

Dealing with a Question of Cultural Boundaries

How would you respond to a question or comment like this?

"A lot of Black people are into crime and drugs, aren't they?"

▶ I think this question is motivated by:

_____

_____

_____

_____

_____

▶ My response to the question would be:

_____

_____

_____

_____

_____

Boundaries—They Don't Fence You In

WITHOUT PERSONAL BOUNDARIES, we have no privacy. Even worse, we can get ourselves entangled in the problems and feelings of others and lose our personal identity. Without cultural boundaries, we lack an informed and positive racial identity. Both types of boundaries are important to growing up Black and proud.

As you get older, it's important to identify your cultural boundaries and to know how to deal with them honestly and in clear, non-defensive, and non-aggressive ways that don't make other people feel stupid or feel that you're judging and condemning them. Remember, other people have boundaries too—personal and cultural. They deserve our respect.

When It Comes to Race, Stay Outta My Face

Cultural/Racial Boundary Areas

THINK ABOUT THE TIMES YOU'VE HAD TO DEAL with cultural boundary issues with others, especially with white people.

Mark with an **O** those issues or situations that have come up with whites when you *OFTEN* felt that race was a factor.

Mark with an **S** those issues or situations that have come up with whites when you *SOMETIMES* felt that race was a factor.

Mark with an **N** those issues or situations that have come up with whites when you felt that race was *NOT* a factor.

____ HUMOR	____ MARRIAGE/DATING
____ HAIR	____ AFFIRMATIVE ACTION
____ CRIME	____ POLITICS
____ SUNBATHING	____ HOUSING/AREAS OF TOWN
____ WELFARE	____ INTELLIGENCE
____ UNEMPLOYMENT	____ ALCOHOL OR OTHER DRUGS
____ ATHLETICS	____ DRESS
____ DANCING	____ STUDENT BEHAVIOR
____ MUSIC	____ BLACK LANGUAGE
____ RELIGION	____ FOOD

____ OTHER: _____

When you finish, go back over the list and look at the issues you marked with an **O**. Circle the three issues that seem to cross cultural boundaries most often.

5

AFRICAN-AMERICAN MALE-FEMALE RELATIONSHIPS

"Love without esteem cannot go far or reach high. It is an angel with only one wing."
Alexander Dumas,
the younger

Bridge-Building

A FRIENDSHIP OR RELATIONSHIP IS LIKE A BRIDGE of understanding between two people. It can't be one-sided. Both people have to build it. Just as a bridge that spans a river needs strong supports, so the relationship bridge between two people needs supports. And what supports a relationship? Shared values.

Think a minute about your *values*. Now look at the supports on the picture of the bridge. In each support write one *value* that you think is necessary to uphold a relationship.

The relationship bridge is paved by shared interests and shared expectations. Look at the eight lines on the bridge pavement. List four *interests* you'd share in a relationship. Then, on the other four lines, list four things you'd *expect* or look for in a relationship.

Black Male-Female Relationships—What's Love Got to Do with It?

PLENTY. BUT JUST WHAT IS "LOVE?" It's the *Number 1* topic of philosophers, poets, and songwriters. In fact, statistics show that "love" is the thirty-sixth word in every song. Big deal? Maybe no, maybe so. It might only mean that "love" sells songs. Or it might mean that "love" is something that's on our minds a lot, that "love" is something we search for, worry over, and wonder about. "What is love?" and "What's love got to do with our relationships with the opposite sex?" These are questions that get asked over and over again. What answers have you come up with so far?

Love Is ...

Put an **X** by any word or phrase below that says what you think love is.

___ freeing

___ recognizing and accepting one another's shortcomings

___ ignoring and denying one another's shortcomings

___ something that takes time and grows only gradually

___ painless

___ blind

___ emotional balance

___ happiness

___ something that happens at first sight

___ emotional ups and downs

___ being taken care of

___ possessing another and his or her time and attention

___ feeling secure

___ sex

___ giving another person all your time

___ painful

___ being concerned about feeling good

___ being concerned about the other person feeling good

___ respectful of another's freedom and uniqueness

___ a relationship that allows a couple to give time to others

___ exhausting; it wipes you out

___ invigorating; it picks you up

Love—Energizing or Draining?

ENERGIZING LOVE TAKES TIME AND EFFORT. It develops slowly. That doesn't mean it's not exciting. It is. Really. Energizing love is fun. It charges you up and makes you feel happy, secure, and joyful. People who have a mature loving relationship really get off being with one another, but they can also deal with being apart.

Draining love can be pretty exciting, too, but it's usually tiring, not energizing. Maybe you've heard someone say, "I can't eat or sleep" or "I can't hang out with you" or "I'm too tired for school." Why? "Because I'm in love!" Draining love wipes people out. Even when they're together, they don't so much enjoy being with one another, as they can't stand being apart.

If you're looking for a relationship that's going to last and lead to real intimacy, you're going to have to be open and caring toward the other person, not just turned on by him or her. Caring deeply for someone of the opposite sex means taking risks together *and* sharing responsibilities together. That takes energy. That takes energizing love.

Becoming the "Sexual" You

YOU ARE A "SEXUAL" PERSON, but your sexuality is more than sex. It's *who you are* and *how you live* as a human being. You relate to other people as a sexual person, a *loving* person—as a woman or as a man who can love and is lovable. This doesn't mean that relationships between the sexes will be easy. You probably already know that they often can be awkward and uncomfortable. Most of us learn to relate to the opposite sex by watching parents, relatives, and other adults who play a part in our growing up. We also get information from movies, television, and music. As we grow older, we begin to learn from firsthand experience.

Sometimes our society has a certain picture of who and what a man or woman should be: girls are "sugar and spice and everything nice"; boys are "squirrels and snails and puppy dog tails." Do you buy that?

Check out the list of qualities below. Circle the ones you want for yourself as a *loving* person.

GENEROUS	CONSIDERATE	CONFIDENT
SHY	ADVENTUROUS	RESPONSIVE
NURTURING	SUBMISSIVE	COMPETITIVE
PERSUASIVE	RELIABLE	SENSITIVE
THOUGHTFUL	DELICATE	SEXY
SMART	ATHLETIC	COURAGEOUS
ASSERTIVE	GIVING	SINCERE

Look over the list again. Mark with an **M** any quality you think society and culture would call masculine. Mark with an **F** any quality that society and culture traditionally call feminine.

Now, see whether the qualities you circled are marked with an **M** or an **F**. The kind of sexual, loving person you want to be is probably a mixture of traditional masculine and feminine traits. And that's good, because your sexuality shouldn't be a cliché. It needs to be based on the kind of behavior *you* believe will make you the happiest now and in the future.

How Race Affects Male-Female Relationships

YOU ALREADY KNOW THAT LOVE can be energizing or exhausting. You know, too, that society has some stereotypes and biases with regard to male-female relationships. Race adds even more. For example, you may feel that most Black men act only in certain ways with women. Likewise, you may feel that Black women act only in certain ways with men. You also may have many questions and stereotypes about men and women from other racial groups, and you may feel that they have stereotypes of you. These thoughts and feelings will make a difference in a number of areas in your life. They'll affect the way you'll answer important questions like the following:

▶ What is love?

▶ What kind of person should I date?

▶ Should I get married someday?

▶ How honest and satisfying will my relationships with the opposite sex be?

Black Men

Read the following statements about African-American men. If you think a statement is *Very True*, mark it with a **V**. If you think a statement is *Somewhat True*, mark it with an **S**. If you think a statement is *Not True At All*, mark it with an **N**.

_____ **1.** Black men are too concerned about sex.

_____ **2.** Black men will not be faithful.

_____ **3.** Black men are loyal.

_____ **4.** Black men would rather be with white women.

_____ **5.** Black men would rather be with light-complexioned women.

_____ **6.** Black men are secure in their masculinity.

_____ **7.** Black men will use women.

_____ **8.** Black men expect women to take care of them.

_____ **9.** Black men are good parents.

_____ **10.** Black men don't value taking care of their families.

_____ **11.** Black men are rarely jealous.

_____ **12.** Black men are irresponsible.

_____ **13.** Black men are good providers.

_____ **14.** Black men are violent.

_____ **15.** Black men are ambitious.

From the above, circle the three statements that you feel are *most true* about Black men.

Black Women

Now read the following statements about African-American women. Again, if you think a statement is *Very True*, mark it with a **V**. If you think a statement is *Somewhat True*, mark it with an **S**. If you think a statement is *Not True At All*, mark it with an **N**.

_____ **1.** Black women are unconcerned about sex.

_____ **2.** Black women don't take care of their bodies.

_____ **3.** Black women are warm and loving.

_____ **4.** Black women are too bossy.

_____ **5.** Black women are poor homemakers.

_____ **6.** Black women are too strict with their children.

_____ **7.** Black women prefer to be with Black men.

_____ **8.** Black women don't expect enough of Black men.

_____ **9.** Black women are jealous of white women.

_____ **10.** Black women are stylish dressers.

_____ **11.** Black women are ambitious.

_____ **12.** Black women are very responsible.

_____ **13.** Black women would rather be with white men.

_____ **14.** Black women are sexier than white women.

_____ **15.** Black women are good parents.

From the above, circle the three statements that you feel are *most true* about Black women.

6

RACISM AND ITS IMPACT

"Some of us came here in a slave boat, others in a steamboat, but we're all in the same boat now."

Jesse Jackson

An Ugly History

THE LONG, PAINFUL, AND TRAGIC HISTORY of racism directed at African Americans and other groups in this country has assumed many forms:

▶ Enslaving African Americans

▶ Interning Japanese Americans during World War II

▶ Massacring American Indians and breaking legal treaties with them

▶ Enacting Jim Crow laws in the South

Understanding racism means recognizing its two key elements:

1. The belief that one racial group is superior to another or others.

2. The ability or power to implement or act on that belief.

Almost all groups of people have practiced one form or another of racism or prejudice. Racism is not unique to just one racial group.

Besides affecting groups of people, racism also has a deeply felt personal impact. It can cause people of color to doubt their abilities and skills, to question each other, to expect *less* of each other. It can make us think that we're not as smart or as pretty as another group. It can rob us of the self-confidence we need to be full and productive human beings. Unfortunately, we can also use the realities of racism as an excuse for our failures and shortcomings, which may, in fact, have nothing to do with race. For example, if we do poorly on a test because we didn't study hard enough, it's often easy to accuse the teacher or the system of being racist or insensitive.

Whenever you see racism rear its ugly head, it's important for you to speak out against it. But it's equally important not to use or present racism as an all-purpose excuse for all your failures and short-comings. Where is the line between these two? Well, it's often difficult to identify. That's why you need to do your best to understand *yourself* as a person of color. Then, when you have to face racism, you can come out the victor, not the victim.

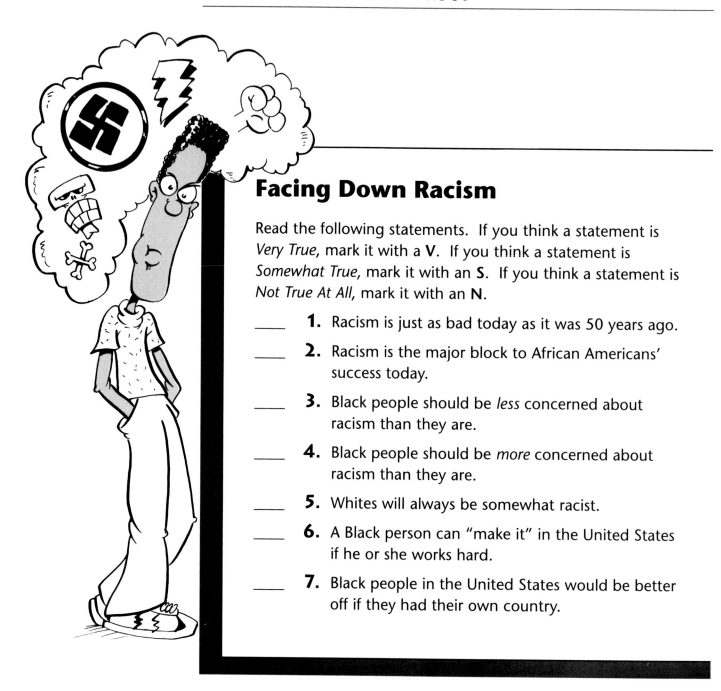

Facing Down Racism

Read the following statements. If you think a statement is *Very True*, mark it with a **V**. If you think a statement is *Somewhat True*, mark it with an **S**. If you think a statement is *Not True At All*, mark it with an **N**.

_____ **1.** Racism is just as bad today as it was 50 years ago.

_____ **2.** Racism is the major block to African Americans' success today.

_____ **3.** Black people should be *less* concerned about racism than they are.

_____ **4.** Black people should be *more* concerned about racism than they are.

_____ **5.** Whites will always be somewhat racist.

_____ **6.** A Black person can "make it" in the United States if he or she works hard.

_____ **7.** Black people in the United States would be better off if they had their own country.

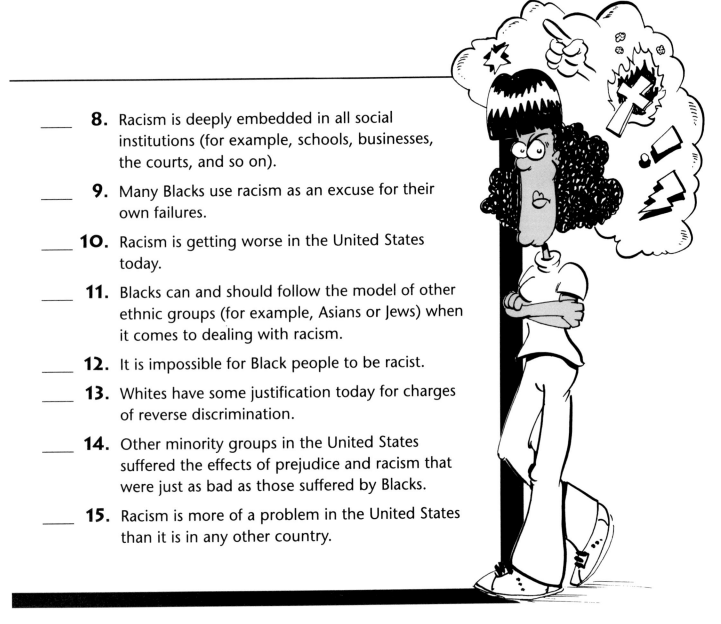

_____ **8.** Racism is deeply embedded in all social institutions (for example, schools, businesses, the courts, and so on).

_____ **9.** Many Blacks use racism as an excuse for their own failures.

_____ **10.** Racism is getting worse in the United States today.

_____ **11.** Blacks can and should follow the model of other ethnic groups (for example, Asians or Jews) when it comes to dealing with racism.

_____ **12.** It is impossible for Black people to be racist.

_____ **13.** Whites have some justification today for charges of reverse discrimination.

_____ **14.** Other minority groups in the United States suffered the effects of prejudice and racism that were just as bad as those suffered by Blacks.

_____ **15.** Racism is more of a problem in the United States than it is in any other country.

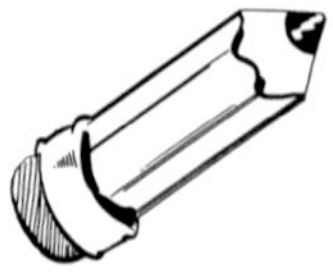

Did you ever find yourself in a position where you had to face down racism? What happened? What did you do? Use the space below to write about it.

_____

_____

_____

_____

_____

_____

_____

_____

_____

_____

_____

_____

_____

_____

_____

_____

_____

_____

_____

7

WHAT IS CHEMICAL DEPENDENCE?

"The person who conceals his disease cannot expect to be set free of it."

Ethiopian Proverb

Chemical Dependence—True or False

Write **T** for true, **F** for false.

_____ **1.** Chemical dependence is a disease.

_____ **2.** Kids your age can become chemically dependent.

_____ **3.** Everyone who uses alcohol or other drugs will become chemically dependent.

_____ **4.** People who are dependent on alcohol or other drugs can stop being dependent if they want to.

_____ **5.** Poor people are more likely to become chemically dependent than rich people.

_____ **6.** Chemical dependence can be cured.

_____ **7.** Chemical dependence always gets worse if the chemically dependent person continues using alcohol or other drugs.

_____ **8.** Black people are more likely to become chemically dependent than white people.

_____ **9.** Luckily, people can't die from chemical dependence.

_____ **10.** Denial makes the chemically dependent person think that alcohol or other drug use is the solution to problems.

_____ **11.** Chemical dependence can't be treated successfully.

_____ **12.** Anyone can become chemically dependent.

What Does It Mean to Be Chemically Dependent?

DO YOU KNOW WHAT CHEMICAL DEPENDENCE IS?
Well, when people are chemically dependent, it means they've lost
their choice and control over how much alcohol or other drugs they
use. People can become chemically dependent on alcohol or on any
other drug.

For example, some people can drink alcohol on special
occasions and stop after one or two drinks. Some people can have a
drink or two every night and stop. But some people keep on
drinking until they become drunk or even after they're drunk. These
people have lost choice and control over how much they drink. And
that's what we call chemical dependence.

People can also lose choice and control over their use of other
drugs like marijuana, heroine, cocaine, and crack. People like that
are also chemically dependent. Anyone can become chemically
dependent: Black, white, rich, poor, women, men, girls, and boys.

Chemical dependence is a disease, just like cancer or diabetes
are diseases. Like any other disease, chemical dependence has certain
tell-tale characteristics:

▶ Primary

▶ Obsessive-Compulsive

▶ Chronic

▶ Progressive and Fatal

▶ Denial

▶ Treatable

Primary. Primary means that even if a chemically dependent person has other problems, the disease of chemical dependence comes first. Even though a chemically dependent person often may have other problems (for example: physical illness, disturbed family relationships, unemployment, problems with police or landlord, trouble at school or at work), none of these problems can be treated effectively until the person stops using alcohol or other drugs. The chemical dependence must be treated first.

Obsessive-Compulsive. Obsessive-compulsive is a big word that means two things at once. First, chemically dependent people think about their drug of choice all of the time. They think about the last time they got high and about the next time they're going to get high. They are *preoccupied* with their drug of choice. Everything they do

centers on getting and using the drug. They spend less time paying attention to family, studies, job, or sports. Alcohol and other drugs become central to the person's life.   Second, the chemically dependent person feels a compulsion, an *irresistible urge* to repeat the same behavior without being able to stop. For the chemically dependent person, the irresistible urge to use alcohol or other drugs is stronger than virtually all other instincts. Once addiction sets in, the person loses the options of choice and control. The chemically dependent person can no more control or choose not to have the disease of chemical dependence than a flu sufferer can control or choose not to have the flu.

Chronic. Chronic means that the disease never goes away and can never be cured. Once people have it, they will always have it. Even if they get help and stop using the drug, they can never use alcohol or any other drug (unless prescribed by a doctor) again, or they will go right back to using to excess.

Progressive and Fatal. Progressive and fatal means that chemical dependence always gets worse if the dependent person continues using alcohol or other drugs. The typical progression goes from using alcohol or other drugs with only a few, minor negative consequences to using them with more and major negative consequences. For example, a chemically dependent person might progress from experiencing a few hangovers, to getting drunk and passing out at a family gathering, to getting picked up repeatedly for driving while intoxicated, to losing a job or getting busted, to becoming physically violent and injuring either himself or herself or someone else.

Chemical dependence is also *fatal*. It can kill people before their time. They die from suicide, or through accidents like falls, car crashes, or overdoses. Or they die from physical illnesses, such as cirrhosis of the liver, that are caused by their use of alcohol or other drugs. Or they die from being a gang member who gets shot while ripping someone off to get drug money. Nasty scenes! Chemical dependence isn't just a bad habit. It's a matter of life or death.

Denial. One of the worst things about chemical dependence is *denial*. Even though a chemically dependent person keeps getting sicker and sicker, the person doesn't realize it because of denial. The chemically dependent person is often the last to know that he or she is sick. The chemically dependent person's denial is very strong. It includes a lot of moves designed to keep the person ignorant of the fact that alcohol or other drug use is the *cause, rather than the solution,* to his or her problems.

Chemically dependent people often blame their problems on other factors such as racism, an unfair teacher, or an unreasonable boss. While these excuses may have some truth to them, the chemically dependent person's other problems will never get solved until his or her number one problem (chemical use) gets solved.

Remember, chemical dependence is the only disease that tells people that they don't have a disease. Denial is a nasty part of the disease and a major road block to recovery.

Treatable. There's some good news in all this. Chemical dependence is *treatable*. Once people admit they have the disease of chemical dependence and decide they want to get better, they can stop using alcohol or other drugs. They might need help from a counselor or a hospital staff trained in chemical dependence. They might also go to self-help groups such as Alcoholics Anonymous or Narcotics Anonymous, or they may go to church again or more often. The chemically dependent person needs to stop using alcohol or other drugs and to change the behavior patterns that he or she developed while using.

So, remember chemical dependence is a disease. Anyone can become chemically dependent. Adults can. Teens can. But remember, too, even if we don't like their behavior, people who are chemically dependent aren't bad people. They're people who are sick and sometimes act bad. If someone you know—a parent or a friend—is chemically dependent, you need to know:

The 3 Cs

1. You didn't <u>Cause</u> the person to develop chemical dependence.

2. You can't <u>Control</u> the person's chemical dependence.

3. You can't <u>Cure</u> or fix the person's chemical dependence.

A Working Definition of Chemical Dependence

_____

_____

_____

_____

_____

_____

_____

8

HOW DOES SOMEONE BECOME CHEMICALLY DEPENDENT?

"Evil enters like a needle and spreads like an oak tree."
Ethiopian Proverb

The Phases of Chemical Dependence:

PHASE 1

PHASE 2

The Sad Adventures of Big D Pendance, Al Kohall, and Kee Rack

PHASE 3

PHASE 4

How to Tell If a Friend or Classmate Is in Trouble with Alcohol or Other Drugs

Section I

YES NO

____ ____ **1.** Has the person ever been arrested on an MIP (Minor In Possession) charge?

____ ____ **2.** Does the person have a poor attitude about school and/or family life?

____ ____ **3.** Is the person becoming less responsible around the house with regard to regular chores or curfews? Has the person ever tried sneaking out of the house at night?

____ ____ **4.** Do most of the person's friends drink alcohol or do other drugs?

____ ____ **5.** Has the person ever had a hangover or a bad trip due to alcohol or other drug use?

____ ____ **6.** Does the person belong to a gang?

____ ____ **7.** Does the person have no job, no rich parent, but a lot of money and a lot of new clothes?

____ ____ **8.** Has the person lied about activities and friends, or made excuses about drinking and other using behaviors?

YES NO

____ ____ **9.** Does the person seem to have unexplainable mood changes or emotional ups and downs that seem too much to you?

____ ____ **10.** Does the person question parents' values about drinking and other drug use? Has the person ever embarrassed his or her parents, you, or others by his or her chemical use? Have you ever covered up or made excuses for the person because of his or her chemical use?

Section II

YES NO

____ ____ **11.** Has the person ever been arrested for shoplifting, vandalism, driving while intoxicated (DWI), or possession of alcohol or other drugs? Has the person ever left empty beer, wine, or liquor bottles, drugs, or drug paraphernalia (papers, pipes, or clips used for holding marijuana cigarettes) lying around?

____ ____ **12.** Has the person ever been suspended from school for possession of alcohol or other drugs or for fighting? Have any of the following occurred frequently: sleeping in school, falling grades, truancy, forging passes, forging excuses about missed classes or days?

____ ____ **13.** Has the person stolen any money or objects from his or her house that could be sold for money? Has the person stolen liquor from parents?   Has the person been fighting or arguing more often with parents? Is the person being more secretive or spending more time in his or her room with the door closed or locked? Has the person been staying out all night?

____ ____ **14.** Has the person changed friends from those who don't use alcohol and other drugs to those who do?

YES NO

____ ____ **15.** Has the person experienced a significant weight loss or gain, unexplained injuries, respiratory problems, or overdoses? Has his or her appearance become sloppy; does he or she seem less concerned with personal hygiene?

____ ____ **16.** Has the person's attention span noticeably decreased? Does he or she have less motivation than in previous times? Does the person blame others more frequently? Has he or she had memory lapses–times when he or she couldn't remember going somewhere or doing something?

____ ____ **17.** Has the person been depressed or voiced feelings of hopelessness and worthlessness? Has the person been saying things like "I wish I were dead" or "Life isn't worth living"?

____ ____ **18.** Has the person pulled away from basic family, educational, or religious values? Has he or she stopped participating in church or family activities?

____ ____ **19.** Does the person strongly defend his or her "right" to drink alcohol or use other drugs?

____ ____ **20.** Have you witnessed the person using others to lie to cover up for himself or herself at school or with friends?

Section III

YES NO

____ ____ **21.** Has the person ever been arrested for robbery, drug dealing, assault and battery, vandalism, or prostitution?

____ ____ **22.** Has the person been suspended from school more than once or expelled? Has he or she been fired from a job?

YES NO

____ ____ **23.** Has the person ever gotten physically violent with you? Has he or she stayed away from home for more than a weekend, or even left home "for good"?

____ ____ **24.** Has the person gotten violent with friends, or started avoiding them to the point where they have begun expressing some concern?

____ ____ **25.** Have you noticed more weight loss or injuries in the person? What about overdoses, tremors, dry heaves, or chronic coughing?

____ ____ **26.** Does the person blame you, family, other friends, and just about anybody else for his or her problems? Are you aware of more times when the person can't seem to remember things that he or she has said or done?

____ ____ **27.** Has the person ever taken part in a crime (for example, armed robbery)?

____ ____ **28.** Does the person seem overwhelmed by despair, self-hatred, or helplessness?

____ ____ **29.** Does the person "turn off" any talk about alcohol and other drug abuse or skip classes about them, dismissing them as "a bore" or "bull"? When confronted with evidence that you know about the person's alcohol or other drug use, does he or she still deny having problems with using?

____ ____ **30.** Are you afraid for the person's safety, or even the person's life, because of any of the behaviors and consequences described in these questions?

Why Use Alcohol and Other Drugs?

LIST REASONS WHY YOU THINK TEENS use alcohol and other drugs.

TOP 10!

REASONS FOR USING

1.
2.
3.
4.
5.
6.
7.
8.
9.
10.

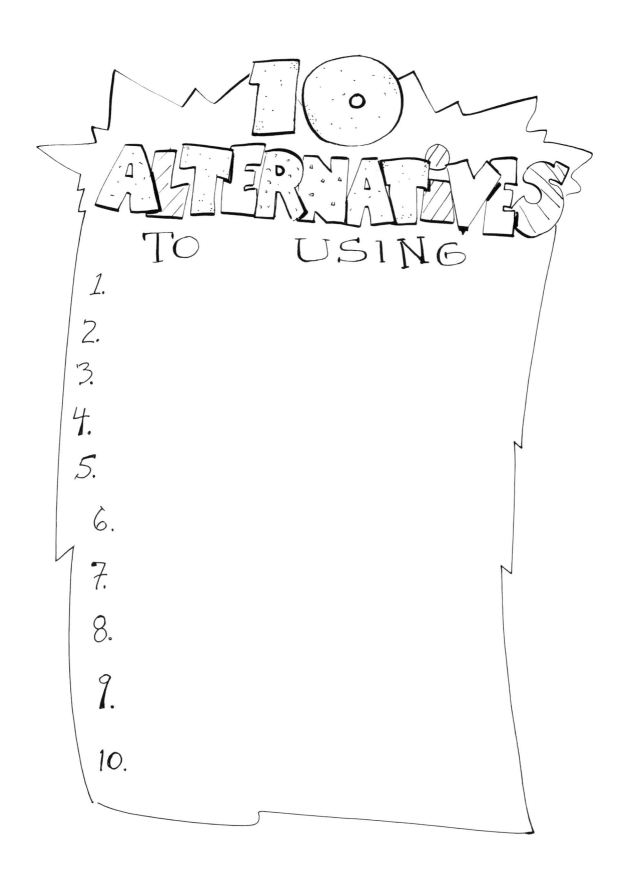

10 ALTERNATIVES TO USING

1.

2.

3.

4.

5.

6.

7.

8.

9.

10.

Why Teens Use Alcohol and Other Drugs— What Adults Say

ADULTS LOOK FOR A CULPRIT. Adults tend to blame ...

It's the schools! They let those kids
get away with anything.

What can you expect from a home like that?
You know what they say, "The acorn
doesn't fall far from the tree."

My kid never had any problems until
he got in with that gang.

Close the bars and lock up the pushers,
and we'd have this thing licked.

5

What do you expect? Kids see the stuff on TV every day.

6

If the cops just nabbed kids the first time they messed up, they could nip this problem in the bud.

7

If the cops would stop treating kids like criminals, they wouldn't even think of using.

8

All those rappers and jocks are into drugs. Some role models!

9

There wouldn't be any problem if those kids just had more job opportunities and society wasn't so racist.

10

Kids need more recreational activities to get them off the street.

Why Teens Use Alcohol and Other Drugs— What Teens Say

TEENS SEEM TO VIEW USING ALCOHOL or other drugs from a different angle. Teens say ...

I wanted to see how I'd feel.

Hey! I'm cool, and I just wanted to have a good time.

I needed to make some cash, you know?

I'm into risks.

5

I do what I wanna do. I'm no kid.

6

I started 'cause there was so much of the stuff around.

7

It was like an experiment, you know?

8

I didn't want to be a square!

9

It's no big deal. Everybody does it.

10

There ain't no future, man! Besides I got a load of pressure at home.

9

HOW CHEMICAL DEPENDENCE AFFECTS FRIENDS, FAMILY AND YOU

"All dope can do for you is kill you ... the long hard way. And it can kill the people you love right along with you."

Billie Holiday

Friendship Diagram

CHECK OUT THE FRIENDSHIP DIAGRAM BELOW.
Write your name in the center circle; write the names of your
friends—past and present—in the other circles. *Note*: You don't have
to fill all the circles.

Show how close you are to your friends by writing one of the
labels listed below on each line leading from the center circle (you) to
the outer circles (your friends): Best Friend; Close Friend; Friend;
Former Friend.

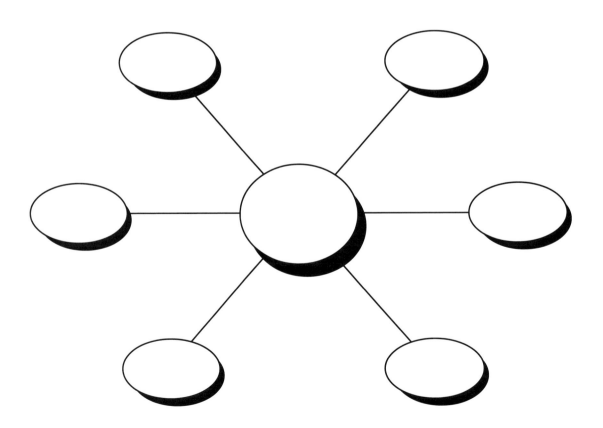

How Chemical Dependence Affects Friendship

ANSWER THESE THREE QUESTIONS ABOUT FRIENDS.

1. What are some things friends your age enjoy doing together?

_____

_____

_____

2. Which of these things, if any, might involve the use of chemicals?

_____

_____

_____

3. How could someone's friendship be affected by the use of chemicals?

_____

_____

_____

How Chemical Dependence Affects the Family

MS. BROWN HAS FOUR HANDSOME CHILDREN and a well-kept apartment in a good neighborhood. She works hard at her job and earns enough money for a modest standard of living. Ms. Brown has a long-time boyfriend named Carl. He spends a lot of time at the Browns' home. He is always there on holidays and has helped to raise the children and pay the bills.   Unfortunately, Carl has become a major problem in the Browns' life. Carl is chemically dependent on alcohol, and his disease is affecting all the Browns.

Ms. Brown has nightmares about her family's future. Each night she goes to bed and each morning she wakes up feeling frightened and angry over Carl's drinking. She fears that he might lose his job. She hates having to call his boss and lie about him being sick with the flu, or a cold, or a sinus headache, or a sore back, or a sprained toe, or an upset stomach, when he is really sick from drinking too much whiskey.

Zazzman, Ms. Brown's eldest child, is an A+ student in school and is captain of the girls' basketball team. Zazzman feels responsible for the problems in her family and hopes to make things all right by doing everything right. She feels that if she can be "perfect," Carl won't drink so much, and he and her mom won't fight so much. Inside, Zazzman feels hurt, confused, guilty, and fearful. Zazzman keeps up this role because it gives her family someone to be proud of.

Reg, Ms. Brown's second child, is a gang member who both sells and uses drugs. He's a poor student and sees no future for himself. He has often stated that he doesn't expect to see his twentieth birthday. He fights constantly with his mother and Carl. Reg figures that if he's bad enough, the family will focus attention on him and deal with him. Then Carl will have to quit drinking. Inside, Reg feels angry, hurt, and abandoned, and he has almost no self-esteem. Reg keeps playing this role because his "bad attitude" keeps the family from focusing on the real problem, Carl's drinking. It also helps Reg feel a false sense of toughness and allows him not to look at his real feelings.

Louie, Ms. Brown's third child, could be nicknamed "the invisible boy." He's way laid-back and spends most of his time alone in his room or buried under headphones. The rest of the family sometimes think that he's a bit out of it. Louie daydreams that he *is* out of it—"it" being his family—and living as the ruler of his own fantasy island somewhere *far* away. Louie figures that if he doesn't make any waves and gets "far enough away," he won't get hurt by Carl's drinking. Inside, however, Louie already feels hurt and abandoned. He believes that he is so unimportant he's not allowed to have feelings. Louie keeps playing this role because it gives some relief to the family and seems to say that everything's really okay.

Moira, Ms. Brown's youngest, is a real pistol. She's an absolutely adorable third grader who's funnier than a stitch. Her goofing off gets her in trouble at school, however, and has sunk her grades somewhere below "C-level." Moira thinks that if she turns everything into a joke, her family will be able to forget about Carl's drinking—at least for awhile. Inside, however, Moira feels absolutely terrified and very unimportant. Moira keeps playing this role because it gives her family comic relief and takes some of the heat off Carl's chemical dependence.

Things are mighty tense around the Brown house. Everyone is trying to control Carl's drinking and actions with different behaviors. Everyone's feeling ticked off, nervous, or scared. But no one talks about these feelings with anyone else. In fact, lately the Browns don't do much of anything with each other. They rarely ever eat together, go to a movie or watch TV together, or have other family times together. They all feel sad, guilty, and lonely inside. All the Browns are blue.

How to Tell If Someone in Your Family Has a Problem with Alcohol or Other Drugs

YES NO

____ ____ **1.** Is the person using more alcohol or other drugs now than in the past?

____ ____ **2.** Are you afraid to be around the person when he or she is drinking or using?

____ ____ **3.** Has the person ever forgotten or denied things that happened when he or she was drinking or using?

____ ____ **4.** Do you worry about the person's drinking or other drug use?

____ ____ **5.** Does the person refuse to discuss his or her drinking or other drug use—or even to discuss the possibility that he or she might have a problem with it?

____ ____ **6.** Has the person broken promises to control or stop?

____ ____ **7.** Has the person ever lied about drinking or using, or tried to hide it from you?

____ ____ **8.** Have you ever been embarrassed by the person's drinking or other drug use?

____ ____ **9.** Have you ever lied to someone else about the person's drinking or other drug use?

____ ____ **10.** Have you ever made excuses for the way the person behaved while drinking or using?

____ ____ **11.** Are many of the person's friends drug users?

____ ____ **12.** Does the person make excuses for the drinking or using?

____ ____ **13.** Do you feel guilty about the person's drinking or other drug use?

YES NO

____ ____ **14.** Are holidays and social functions often unpleasant for you because of the person's drinking or other drug use?

____ ____ **15.** Do you feel nervous or tense around the person because of his or her drinking or other drug use?

____ ____ **16.** Have you ever helped the person "cover up" for drinking or using (for example, by calling the person's boss or by telling others he or she is sick)?

____ ____ **17.** Does the person deny having a drinking problem because he or she drinks only beer or wine? Or deny having another drug problem because use is "limited" to marijuana, diet pills, a few lines of "coke," or some other supposedly "harmless" drug?

____ ____ **18.** Does the person's behavior change when he or she is drinking or using? (For example, a normally quiet person might become loud, or a normally mild-mannered person might become quick to anger.)

____ ____ **19.** Does the person avoid social functions at which alcohol or other drugs *won't* be available?

____ ____ **20.** Does the person insist on going only to restaurants or clubs that serve alcohol?

____ ____ **21.** To your knowledge, has the person ever driven a car while under the influence of alcohol or other drugs?

____ ____ **22.** Has anyone else ever talked to you about the person's using or drinking behavior?

____ ____ **23.** Has the person ever expressed sorrow for the way he or she behaved while drinking or using?

____ ____ **24.** Does the person seem to have a low self-image?

____ ____ **25.** Have you ever found alcohol or other drugs that the person has hidden?

____ ____ **26.** Does the person seem to be having money or work problems that are linked to alcohol or other drug use?

____ ____ **27.** Does the person look forward to times when he or she can drink alcohol or use other drugs?

____ ____ **28.** Do you sometimes feel responsible for the person's drinking or drug use, or that you may be the cause of it?

What If You Live with Someone Who Is Chemically Dependent?

IF YOU LIVE WITH SOMEONE who's chemically dependent, you have to understand that the situation is one you *can't* change and that chemical dependence is a problem you *can't* solve. But, you can take some steps to help you deal with it.

First off, remember that you can ask for help, and it's always okay to ask for help. Check with trusted adults or friends. There's absolutely nothing wrong with taking care of yourself first. Taking care of yourself is self-preservation. It's not selfishness. If the chemically dependent person is an adult, remember that it's not your job to fix the adult's problems. Adults should take care of their own problems. An adult may need to ask for help, and it's okay for an adult to ask for help, too.

The disease of chemical dependence messes up the way people act, think, feel, and how they treat others. They say and do things they don't really mean. For example, a chemically dependent parent may call you a rotten kid, hit you, or blame his or her chemical use on you. DON'T YOU BELIEVE IT! That's the alcohol or other drug talking, hitting, and blaming. You can't control a chemically dependent person's actions, but you can control *yours*. You can do something that makes you feel better, like listen to some tunes, shoot some hoops, talk to a trusted friend. If you think you should talk to the chemically dependent person about your feelings, remember to wait until the person is sober.

Marla's Coping Strategy

A COPING STRATEGY IS A PLAN or way to handle a problem you can't change or solve. Marla has come up with a coping strategy to help her handle the problem of her mom's drinking. Whenever Marla's mom drinks alcohol, she ends up fighting with her husband. Marla hates it when her parents argue and fight, so Marla worked out this coping strategy to help deal with the problem:

1. She realizes and accepts that she can't make her parents stop fighting. It's not her job, and she wouldn't succeed anyway.

2. She makes plans to go to a safe place where she won't get hurt. For example, her neighbor's apartment, or the local youth center.

3. She decides to listen to her favorite song to help her feel better.

Your Coping Strategy

LET'S SUPPOSE YOU HAPPEN TO BE LIVING with someone who's chemically dependent. Let's also suppose that when that person gets drunk or high he or she picks on you and yells at you. What will you do? What sort of coping strategy would help you?

Go back and read over "What If You Live with Someone Who Is Chemically Dependent?" again. Check out the coping ideas there. Then write down three things you would do to help you deal with living with someone who's chemically dependent.

1._____

_____

_____

_____

2._____

_____

_____

_____

3._____

_____

_____

_____

10

HOW CHEMICAL DEPENDENCE AFFECTS THE AFRICAN-AMERICAN COMMUNITY

"Not to know is bad. Not to want to know is worse."
Proverb of West Africa

The Chain of Problems

LIKE OTHER COMMUNITIES, the Black community has problems. They include the following:

▶ Dropping out of school

▶ Crime

▶ Teen pregnancy

▶ High unemployment

▶ Low-skilled workforce

▶ Illiteracy

▶ Poverty

▶ Single-parent families

▶ Poor housing

▶ HIV/AIDS

▶ Other: _____

Many African-American leaders are reminding us that if we're not part of the solution, we're part of the problem. Their warnings are important because many Blacks are trying to escape their community's problems by turning to alcohol and other drugs. Not only does this do nothing to solve the problems in the Black community, it creates more.

Think a minute about what people do when they use alcohol or other drugs. Remember, alcohol and other drugs mess up judgment. They screw up the way people act, think, feel, and how they treat others. People who are drunk or high do things they might never do while sober. People using alcohol or other drugs are more likely to:

▶ | Have sex outside of marriage and have unprotected sex

▶ | Physically abuse others

▶ | Commit crimes

▶ | Ignore responsibilities, such as: doing homework, going to work or school, supporting and taking care of kids, keeping promises

▶ | Neglect their health and the health of loved ones, especially those they're responsible for

▶ | Other: _____

Chemical Dependence— Problem #1

Do you recall how we discovered that chemical dependence is a *primary* disease? "Primary" *doesn't mean* that chemical dependence always causes all the other problems in someone's life or community. "Primary" *doesn't mean* that it's the most important problem in someone's life or community. But "primary" *does mean* that chemical dependence is a problem that must be dealt with *first*. Why? Alcohol and other drugs are real "mind messers." They mess up thinking *bad*. Someone who's hooked on alcohol or other drugs can't focus on other problems, because his or her judgment is twisted. The chemically dependent person has to deal with his or her addiction *first*. Otherwise, no other problems are going to get solved.

MALCOLM'S PROBLEM

Malcolm is unemployed—has been for awhile. He's also an alcoholic. Malcolm's wife is on his case to quit drinking, get off welfare, and find a job. Malcolm says that his #1 problem is being unemployed. He figures that if he could land a job he'd be just fine.
What do you think?

VANESSA'S PROBLEM

Vanessa dropped out of school when she was 16. She made a few bucks by selling crack and then started using it herself. Now she's dependent on it. She can't find a job and wants to go back to school. Vanessa says that her #1 problem is the fact that she dropped out. She thinks that if she could get back in school, everything would be better. **What do you think?**

PERCY'S PROBLEM

Percy is angry at whites. Every time he feels himself getting ticked off, he smokes some reefer. The stuff mellows him out and lets him escape for awhile. Percy says that his #1 problem is the racism that holds him down as a Black man. He thinks that if Blacks could get more power, all his troubles would be over. **What do you think?**

NAOMI'S PROBLEM

Naomi is a heroin addict. Two months ago she tested HIV positive and is now carrying around the AIDS virus. Naomi is scared. She's still using heroin every day, still sharing needles, and still having sex. Naomi says that her #1 problem is the AIDS virus. She figures that if she can get some good treatment for her HIV, life would get a whole lot better for her. **What do you think?**

"No Problem!"

ON THE EARLY DAYS OF THE OLD "COSBY SHOW," whenever the son (Theo) came up against some difficulty, his response was "No problem!" Well, that's *the* slogan of chemically dependent people. Remember, chemical dependence is a "disease of denial." People who are hooked on alcohol or other drugs rarely admit it. They say, "No problem. I can quit any time." Then they turn around and give you all kinds of excuses why they continue to use. In fact, they use other problems as reasons or excuses for using:

▶ ▍ If I had a job, I wouldn't drink.

▶ ▍ If I had a better education, I wouldn't do crack.

▶ ▍ If society wasn't so racist, I wouldn't smoke marijuana.

▶ ▍ If I didn't have AIDS, I wouldn't shoot heroin.

The truth is, most chemically dependent people *can't* stop using without some help. Just the thought of quitting booze or laying off marijuana or forgetting crack or stopping heroin scares people who are dependent on these drugs half to death. They've gotten used to ducking problems by turning to chemicals. In fact, they look on alcohol or other drugs as "best partners." They can't imagine life without them and the escape from real life they provide.

No problem? You bet there's a problem. When alcohol and other drugs are best partners, they ruin health, cost people time and money, and keep them from dealing with important issues and problems in their personal *and* in their community lives.

What's the Problem Here?

DON'T GO THINKING THAT BECAUSE we're talking about chemical dependence and the Black community that it's the *only* community with the problem. The Black community is not the only community with problems. Nor is it the only community that has a problem with alcohol or other drugs. We're talking about this because we want to be proud of our community. We want to face up to our problems; as the West African proverb says, "Not to know is bad. Not to want to know is worse." We want to know our problems so that our community can gain the strength to deal with them. We don't want chemical dependence to make our problems worse or to keep us from dealing with them.

Discussion Guide

My Group's "Community" Problem:

_____

Describe the Problem:

_____

_____

_____

_____

How Alcohol and Other Drugs Affect the Problem:

Do they help? How?

_____

_____

_____

Do they complicate or add to the problem? How?

_____

_____

_____

_____

_____

_____

11

COMMUNICATING

"I don't let my mouth say nothin' my head can't stand."

Louis Armstrong

What's the big deal about communication? It's only talking, right? Wrong! Babies communicate without talking. Hearing-impaired people communicate without talking and hearing. Real communication doesn't mean just talking, or even talking and hearing. Real communication means giving and receiving information. And we do that in a lot of ways.

List some ways you communicate:

1. _____

2. _____

3. _____

4. _____

The Goal of Communication

WHY IS IT IMPORTANT ...

▶ to say the right thing to that man or lady you think is so fine?

▶ to keep in contact with your friends?

▶ to pay attention when a brother or sister asks you something?

▶ to help others understand what you're feeling?

▶ to look cool?

▶ to let other people know what you need?

▶ to let others know what you're doing or where you're going?

▶ to speak up for yourself?

We communicate for one basic reason—*to connect with others.* We all want connections. We all want our friends and other people to understand us. Well, people can't read our minds. In order to let them know who we are, what we want, or how we're feeling, we need to communicate. We need to connect with others.

Now remember, communicating is always two-sided. Even if we do a good job trying to connect with someone, that doesn't mean that person is going to let us make the connection. The other person might not really "hear" us or might refuse to pay attention to us. We can't control how others communicate with us, but we can control how we communicate with them.

Making Connections

There are six guidelines that can help you communicate well and make connections with others. The first four have to do with "giving" information. The last two deal with "receiving" information.

1. No jiving.

2. Expect to be treated with respect.

3. Treat others with respect.

4. Stay cool.

5. Pay attention to the message being delivered.

6. Give both verbal and nonverbal feedback.

No jiving. This is what Louis Armstrong meant when he said, "I don't say nothin' my head can't stand." B.S.-ing others is B.S.-ing yourself. If you figure that what you're telling other people stinks, you're figuring right. Others can smell it too! B.S.-ing people sends only one message and sends it loud and clear: "I'm full of it!"

Expect to be treated with respect. Aretha Franklin was right on. Everyone needs respect. If you're doing your best to be honest with others, you have a right to expect to be listened to. What you have to say is important. Otherwise you wouldn't be saying it, right? So, don't be afraid to speak up for yourself and tell others what you want and need. If you don't, you'll never connect.

Treat others with respect. This is the flip side of the respect coin. If you want respect from others, you have to respect them. They have their own ideas, opinions, needs, and wants to communicate, and these might be different from yours. That doesn't make *them* wrong. Nor does it make *you* wrong. It just makes you two different people who need to communicate.

Communicating with Respect

One of the best ways to get and give respect when communicating is to use "I statements." I statements let you be outspoken without being loudmouthed.

I statements let you stay focused on improving yourself or your situation rather than gossiping about others or tripping on them. I statements let you stick up for yourself, say no to difficult situations, express how you feel, or ask for what you need without judging or dissing or capping on the person you're trying to communicate with. Check out these I statements:

▶ "I feel angry when you pressure me for sex because I'm just not ready for that sort of relationship."

▶ "I need more time to finish my homework because I had trouble understanding the reading."

▶ "I feel scared when you sell crack because you're my friend, and I don't want you to get in trouble."

Practice using I statements when you communicate. They can help you connect honestly and respectfully with others.

Stay cool. If you really want to blow a communication, blow up. Nothing disconnects people better than uncontrolled anger. When we express anger in an "uncool," violent way, the other person can respond only in one of two ways: with anger or with fear. And there is no such thing as a real relationship based on either anger or fear. In our next session, we'll be dealing more with ways we express feelings like anger. For now, remember that none of us can really communicate with someone who's in our face.

Pay attention to the message being delivered. When we're "receiving" information from someone, the first thing we have to do is pay attention. This means more than simply hearing what's being said or communicated. It means understanding it. So, if you don't understand, ask questions. Have the person repeat. Make sure you "get" what the other is "giving."

Give both verbal and nonverbal feedback. Feedback furthers communication. It tells the other person that he or she is or isn't getting through. A positive nod of the head, an encouraging "I see what you mean," or a reflecting "Let me get this straight," all support effective communication and help connect us with the other person.

Broken Connections

WHAT HAPPENS WHEN COMMUNICATIONS between groups or individuals break down? Two things: Anger and loneliness.

Anger. In 1992, communications between the African-American community and the white community of Los Angeles, California, suffered a major breakdown. The voices, needs, and feelings of African Americans had long gone unheard. When a jury acquitted a group of white policemen of brutally beating a black man—a beating seen by millions on videotape—the unheard voices of African Americans in Los Angeles, and in other U.S. cities, exploded into anger, violence, and riot. As Dr. Martin Luther King Jr. once said, "A riot is the language of the unheard."

Loneliness. When Carver could not get through to Felicia to let her know how he felt about her, he began to feel lonely. No matter how hard he tried, he just couldn't seem to connect with her and get a relationship going. Pretty soon Carver started feeling like a real failure. His loneliness got worse. He turned to drinking wine and then to smoking crack to feel better. Instead, Carver became even more withdrawn and isolated. In a very short time, the only communicating Carver was doing was with his pusher, and the only relationship he had left was with dope.

12

DEALING WITH FEELINGS

"If you're not feeling good about you, what you're wearing on the outside doesn't mean a thing."

Patti LaBelle

Kujichagulia

KUJICHAGULIA (COO-GEE-CHA-GOO-LEE-AH) is a Swahili word that means "self-determination" or thinking for yourself. Many African Americans see kujichagulia as one of the Nguzo Saba (n-GOO-zoh SAH-ba) or Principles of Blackness. By now, you know that alcohol and other drugs can really mess up your kujichagulia. Why? Because people who are chemically dependent let chemicals do their thinking for them.

SCOPE THIS OUT:

Dedric isn't doing so hot. Keesha, his girl, just dumped him. So Dedric's walking around with a whole bunch of feelings all balled up inside. His stomach feels tight. His head aches and his back hurts. Dedric needs help dealing with his feelings, but he can't talk to anyone. No way he's going to admit he's been dissed. Besides, he wouldn't know what to say even if he could talk about the way he's feeling.

After school, Dedric spots Allan. Everyone at school knows that Allan is always holding some marijuana or crack. Dedric starts talking to Allan; pretty soon he tells him he'd like to get high. Allan shares a joint with Dedric. Before they split, Allan sells Dedric two marijuana joints and a rock of crack.

Whoa! Why did Dedric so easily turn to chemicals? If you think it's because Keesha left him, you're only partly right. The deeper reason Dedric started using has to do with not being able to deal with all the feelings that are bottled up inside him. And, because he can't deal with his feelings, Dedric has chosen to let chemicals change his feelings and to give up his kujichagulia and let marijuana and crack do his thinking for him. Whether Dedric gets back together with Keesha or not, what he needs most is to develop ways to deal with feelings that don't involve alcohol or other drugs.

In the space below, write down the names of the feelings you think Dedric might have been having.

Questioning Feelings

▶ Why do you think kids like Dedric have a hard time talking about feelings?

▶ What role does keeping a cool image play in the way we deal with feelings?

▶ How do kids your age describe people who express their feelings—feelings like loneliness, sadness, inadequacy, and so on?

Naming Feelings

WHEN IT COMES TO DEALING WITH FEELINGS, the best place to start is learning to name them. "Good" or "bad" are *not* names of feelings. They're judgment calls about feelings. Feelings aren't good or bad. Feelings just *are.* You can't control what feelings you get. That's why it's always okay to feel the way you feel. However, it's not always easy to name what you're feeling. But you can do something about that. You can expand your dictionary of feelings. Check out these names of feelings.

AFRAID	DISAPPOINTED	HOPEFUL	POWERFUL/LESS
AGGRESSIVE	DISCOURAGED	HOPELESS	PROUD
AMUSED	ENTHUSIASTIC	HURT	REJECTED
ANGRY	ENVIOUS	INSPIRED	RELIEVED
ANXIOUS	EXCITED	INSECURE	SAD
APPRECIATED	FRIGHTENED	JEALOUS	SAFE
BORED	FRUSTRATED	JOYFUL	TENSE
COMFORTABLE	FURIOUS	LONELY	UNLOVED
CONCERNED	GLAD	LOVED	WANTED
CONFUSED	GUILTY	MISERABLE	WORTHLESS
CONTENTED	HAPPY	NERVOUS	WORTHWHILE

Quite the list, huh? And there are many other feeling words, too.

▶ ▎ From the list above, circle the feeling(s) you recall having during the past week.

▶ ▎ Underline any of the feelings Dedric might have had.

▶ ▎ What does it mean to *name* feelings?

Claiming Feelings

ONCE YOU START GETTING THE HANG OF naming your feelings, the next step is to *claim* them. Your feelings are *yours*, no one else's. They're part of *you*. Too often we blame our feelings—especially our uncomfortable feelings—on other people, or we hold others responsible for the way we feel. For example, kids who live with a chemically dependent person often say, "I feel angry because my mom does cocaine" or "I feel sad because my dad gets drunk" or "It's my friend's responsibility to make me feel happy."

If you've ever said or thought like that, remember, the feelings you have are *your* feelings. They belong to *you*. You need to claim them as yours.

If you don't claim your feelings and take responsibility for them, you're giving up control over your life. You're allowing others to decide how you're going to feel *and* act. Claiming your feelings lets you see what's behind them and what they might be signaling you to do. For example, suppose a parent's drug use gives you an uncomfortable feeling. Then, let's say that you *name* that feeling as anger. By *naming*, then *claiming* that feeling of anger as your own, you may discover that it is signaling you to do something about your uncomfortable situation—to make some positive changes *for yourself*. You can't always control how you feel, but you *can* control how you act or react.

FEELINGS CAN BE

_____ AND _____

BUT NEVER _____.

Communicating/ Expressing Feelings

ONE OF THE WORST THINGS YOU CAN DO is to keep your feelings bottled up inside. Feelings need to be communicated and expressed—shared with someone. If this doesn't happen, you'll end up alone and cut off from the support and concern of others. You can express feelings in a lot of ways: through poetry, music, sports, art, writing, or even yelling. Still, it's pretty important to find ways to communicate feelings to others. You need to say out loud, "I feel confused when you treat me like that" or "I feel angry when you get drunk and break your promises to me." If you don't find appropriate ways to express your feelings, you'll end up frustrated and cut off from others. You might even find yourself acting in ways that mess you up bad. Remember Dedric? He expressed his feelings in a way that could really hurt him—by doing drugs.

Feelings are natural and normal. You shouldn't "diss" yourself about your feelings or "diss" others about theirs. You can't control the feelings you get, but you can learn to control your behavior—the way you communicate or express your feelings. By naming and claiming your feelings, you can put some new thinking between what you feel and how you act. For example, if a parent is chemically dependent and is feeling angry, you don't have to feel angry and then act angrily, too. Instead, you can do some new thinking before you act: "I can't be responsible for the way my mom feels. My mom feels angry, but *I* don't have to feel angry. I'm different from my mom. I'm responsible for *my* feelings. If I *do* feel angry, I can choose to express that feeling in a way that will help me feel better."

How would you express anger in a way that would help you feel better?

When it comes to communicating/expressing feelings, "I statements" are a great way to go.

"I feel _____ when _____, because

_____. "

    Example: *"I feel hurt when you use cocaine, because it makes you forget the promises you've made to me."*

Fleeting Feelings

THERE'S ONE LAST THING YOU SHOULD KNOW about feelings. Feelings come and go. No one is happy all of the time, or angry all of the time, or sad all of the time. Feelings are temporary and passing. This is important to remember when you're experiencing the ups and downs of becoming an adult. Feelings *will* change. You can count on it.

▶ Think of a feeling you had during the past week (for example, inadequate, lonely, happy, sad).

_____

_____

▶ Why did you have that feeling?

_____

▶ What might that feeling have been signalling you to do?

_____

_____

▶ What might be some appropriate ways you could express that feeling?

_____

_____

_____

CHILLing Anger—
What's Worth Saving?
Your Face or Your Life?

HOW MANY TIMES HAVE YOU SEEN FIGHTS START when a couple of kids get heated up over the dozens? How many times have you heard of someone getting shot over a pair of shoes, a team cap, a sports jacket, or a remark made about someone else's mamma? Why does this happen and continue to happen, especially in the African-American community?

It happens because too many African-American kids are willing to risk their lives rather than to lose face. It happens because too many African-American kids feel pressured to express their anger in violent ways just to look cool in front of their friends.

But it's totally uncool to always blow your cool. Worse, it can be dangerous to others and to yourself. When you feel anger like a fire in your belly, it's okay to express it, but not with acts of violence. Instead, take time to CHILL.

Choose forceful words, but not fighting words, to express your anger.

Hear that your anger is signalling you to make some changes. You can use your anger to give the power you need to make changes.

Interrupt your anger. Stop to give yourself some time to think before expressing your angry feelings.

Leave. This is not the same as running from or bottling up anger. Rather, it's seeing that anger is like a hot and fiery wind. Leaving means getting out of the way before anger blows you or someone else over. You may lose face now and then, but you also may save your life or someone else's.

Listen to the way your anger is signalling you to make *positive* changes (for example, to solve a problem or to resolve a conflict).

The Feelings Equation

WHEN IT COMES TO ATOMIC POWER, this is the equation that matters: $E=mc^2$

When it comes to matters of feelings, this is the equation that empowers:

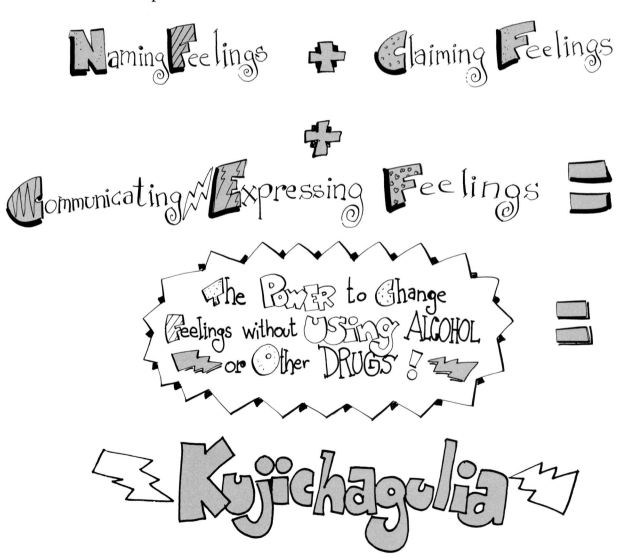

Naming Feelings **+** Claiming Feelings

+

Communicating/Expressing Feelings **=**

The Power to Change Feelings without Using Alcohol or Other Drugs! **=**

Kujichagulia

13

MAKING DECISIONS/ SOLVING PROBLEMS/ RESOLVING CONFLICTS

"A problem is a chance for you to do your best."

Duke Ellington

Working Through Problems

EVERY DAY YOU HAVE DECISIONS TO MAKE and problems to solve. You have to decide what to wear, what and when to eat, which way to take to get to school or a job, what time to get up, what time to go to bed. Over time, through trial and error and your life experiences, you've already learned to work through lots of different problems.

Sometimes, however, more difficult problems might come your way, such as whether to shoplift, skip or quit school, get involved sexually with someone, or use alcohol or other drugs. When you're confronted with tough problems, it's cool to have a way of working through them that you can rely on. Check out these steps for working through problems:

1. Identify the problem.

(*What's the real problem here?*)

2. Name and claim responsibility for how you feel about the problem.

(*How do I feel about it?*)

3. Identify possible choices.

(*What can I do?*)

4. Examine possible consequences.

(*If I do this, what might happen next?*)

5. Select the best possible solution.

(*What is the* best *thing to do?*)

6. Carry out the solution.

(*Now, do it!*)

7. Evaluate the action and its consequences.

(*Did the solution I chose solve the problem?*)

8. Evaluate the success of your problem solving.

(*What can I do to reward myself for solving the problem or change my strategy to be more effective?*)

Deciding What to Do

READ THROUGH THE FOLLOWING FIVE PROBLEMS. See if you can use the eight-step problem-solving plan to help you decide what to do.

1. After basketball practice, some of your team members are huddled together, passing around a joint. They tell you that they're doing it for a thrill and to mellow out after the rough practice. They offer you a hit. Decide what to do.

2. It's Wednesday. You have tickets for an R&B concert on Thursday night. They cost a bundle, and you've been looking forward to the concert for a month. Your math teacher announces that there's going to be a test on Friday. It will count for fifty percent of your grade. You know that if you blow this test, it's summer school for sure. You need a good grade on Friday's test, but you really want to go to the concert Thursday night. Now what?

3. You're new in school and have trouble feeling "in." The only kids who pay any attention to you are "thugs." They've asked you three times to hang out with them after school. So far, you've managed to come up with excuses not to go, but you really want to have some new friends. They've asked you to a party next Saturday night. How will you handle this one?

4. For an upcoming dance, all your best friends are planning to wear the same style outfit. You already have your outfit and don't have enough money to buy a new one to be like your friends. Decide what to do.

5. Your parents are leaving town for the weekend. You'll be home alone. They specifically told you not to have friends over and NO parties. Your friends tell you that they're coming over with some tapes and some wine. How will you deal with this situation?

Resolving Conflicts

NO MATTER HOW YOU LOOK AT THEM, conflicts are messy situations. Very often they lead to anger, violence, and hurt. That's why most of us try to avoid conflicts. But in the real world, conflicts *do* happen. Other values clash with ours. People get in our faces. Then what? How do we deal with or resolve conflicts?

Generally, there are three ways of resolving conflicts:

> ▶ **LOSE/LOSE**
>
> ▶ **WIN/LOSE**
>
> ▶ **WIN/WIN**

CHECK OUT THE FOLLOWING EXAMPLES:

LOSE/LOSE: *Yolanda can't find her new pen. She notices that Amahd, who sits next to her in class, is using it, and she feels really ticked. "Hey, nigger," she yells, "you copped my pen! Hand it over!" Surprised and angry himself, Amahd responds, "Sez you, bitch. I found it on the floor." Yolanda reaches over, slaps Amahd and grabs the pen out of his hand. He tries to snatch it back and ends up knocking over Yolanda's desk with her in it. At this point the teacher steps in and sends them both to the principal's office where they both get detention. Yolanda and Amahd don't speak to each other and stay angry at each other for a week.*

WIN/LOSE: *Yolanda can't find her new pen. She notices that Amahd, who sits next to her in class, is using it and feels really ticked. "Hey," she yells, "you copped my pen! Hand it over!" Amahd doesn't even look up, but he responds, "Sez you. This is my pen." Yolanda says, "No way, man! See the 'Y.G.' on it? Those are my initials. So give it back, okay?" Amahd turns to Yolanda and snarls, "Just back off, unless you're lookin' for a world of trouble." Fearful, Yolanda digs out a pencil from her book bag. She goes home that night, avoiding Amahd, feeling angry at him and determined to get even.*

WIN/WIN: *Yolanda can't find her new pen. She notices that Amahd, who sits next to her in class, is using it and feels really ticked. "Hey," she yells, "you copped my pen! Hand it over!" Amahd looks up and responds, "Relax. This ain't your pen. It's mine." Yolanda says, "No way, man! See the 'Y.G.' on it? Those are my initials. So give it back, okay?" Amahd checks out the initials, then says, "Oh, it is yours. I guess I picked it up by mistake. Here." Yolanda begins to smile and says, "My dad gave it to me on my sixteenth birthday." Amahd smiles back. "Only problem is, I don't have a pen to finish this paper," Amhad says. Yolanda begins scrounging around in her book bag, finds an old ballpoint, and hands it to Amahd. "Keep it," Yolanda says.*

Coming Out on Top of Conflicts— The Win/Win Solution

HERE'S HOW TO RESOLVE CONFLICTS so that both parties come out winners.

1. Take time to CHILL. Find alternative ways to express angry feelings. Don't say or do anything to make the problem worse.

2. Have each person identify the problem as he or she sees it. Don't blame or accuse. Instead, use "I statements."

3. Each person identifies what part he or she plays in the problem and identifies what part he or she thinks the other person plays.

4. Include both parties in the problem-solving steps to arrive at a compromise, a solution that both can live with.

5. Note how each party cooperated to resolve the conflict and congratulate one another.

"If you allow the law of 'an eye for an eye,' very soon, the only people around are going to be blind."

Bishop Desmond M. Tutu

My Safety Net

People to talk to when I feel angry, have a tough
problem, or am in conflict with someone:

_____

_____

_____

People I can go to so I feel safe:

_____

_____

_____

People I can have fun with:

_____

_____

_____

Other people I can ask for help:

_____

_____

_____

Important telephone numbers:

_____

_____

14

DEALING WITH PEER PRESSURE

"Love yourself and your kind."
Elijah Muhammed

Being "In" the Peer Pressure Cooker

EVERY TEEN WANTS TO BE "IN," to be tight with others. That's cool. That's normal. But being "in" might also mean being caught in a peer pressure cooker—feeling forced to do things you don't want to do or to be someone you're not. Being "in" costs. How much do you think kids your age are willing to pay? Look at the following list. Rank the items, 1 to 10, according to what you think kids your age would be willing to give up to pay the cost of being "in." Let number 1 be the first thing kids might give up, number 10, the last.

____ Style of clothes

____ Favorite music

____ Good looks

____ Self-respect

____ Religious values and beliefs

____ Attitude toward school

____ Loyalty to family

____ Hairstyle

____ Loyalty to the Black community

____ Honesty

Fear: *The* "F" Word

THERE'S NOTHING WRONG WITH WANTING TO BE "in" and liked, unless we have to pay too high a price for it. But a lot of us are willing to pay that price, no matter how high. Ever wonder why? The answer is because we're afraid. And we're fearful for a lot of different reasons.

Fear of Being Blown Off

WHEN IT COMES TO BEING PART OF THE GROUP, fear of rejection can really mess you up. If you're afraid of being blown off by others, you might have to pay the price of never being the real you. Instead, you'll spend your time wearing a mask: "the clown," "the brain," "the fox," "the hard ass," "the cool dude," or whatever. And walking around wearing a mask means covering up some of your best qualities.

Fear of rejection stops you from letting others know what you're really like and what you really enjoy. It can also turn you into someone you're not. Some people may like you, but they'll like you for all the wrong reasons.

Circle the number that best describes the amount of fear of rejection you believe African-American kids your age are feeling.

1   2   3   4   5   6   7   8   9   10

NONE   A LITTLE   SOME   A LOT   SCARED STIFF

Fear of Getting Hurt

FEAR OF GETTING HURT can turn you into an "avoider," and avoiders can never really be "in," because they can never be a true friend to anyone. Remember, true friends share everything—painful things as well as happy things. Fear of getting hurt also has a way of coming back at you and screwing you up. When you do things to be liked, just in order to avoid pain, you almost always make someone else suffer, and probably yourself as well.

Let's get real, okay? If you want to be liked for who you really are, there's going to be some hurt involved. You may not like it, but that's the way life is.

Circle the number that best describes the amount of fear of getting hurt you believe African-American kids your age are feeling.

1   2   3   4   5   6   7   8   9   10

NONE   A LITTLE   SOME   A LOT   SCARED STIFF

Fear of Failing

FEAR OF FAILING OR BEING A LOSER comes from worrying that others will judge you not according to who you are, but on what you do or achieve. Fear of failing can really bring you down. It can stop you from taking the risk to meet or care for others: "If I ask him to go to the movies and he says 'no,' I won't be able to show my face in school." Fear of failing can make you feel worthless if you don't succeed: "If I don't make the varsity b'ball team, all the brothers will think I'm a chump." Worst of all, fear of failing can stop you from trying new things: "I really want to try out this new dance at the talent show, but I better not 'cause I might mess up."

Fear of failing can be paralyzing. No one wants to fumble in front of friends.

Circle the number that best describes the amount of fear of failure you believe African-American kids your age are feeling.

1	2	3	4	5	6	7	8	9	10
NONE	**A LITTLE**			**SOME**		**A LOT**		**SCARED STIFF**	

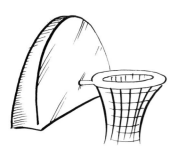

Fear of Being Alone

IF YOU'RE LOOKING FOR A FUNDAMENTAL FEAR, loneliness is probably it. Fear of being alone can make people do some pretty dumb things in order to be liked: lie to a friend, act with prejudice toward a group or a race, get involved in alcohol and other drugs, or betray one's values or race.

Listen, you're going to feel lonely now and then—*for sure*. So don't let feelings of loneliness trouble you or freak you out. Most of all, don't let fear of loneliness turn you into a phony, someone who acts one way or does things just to be "in." A phony is the loneliest person there is.

Circle the number that best describes the amount of fear of loneliness or being alone you believe African-American kids your age are feeling.

1	**2**	**3**	**4**	**5**	**6**	**7**	**8**	**9**	**10**
NONE		**A LITTLE**		**SOME**		**A LOT**		**SCARED STIFF**	

The Remarkably Likeable You

YOU WANT TO BE LIKED "JUST FOR YOURSELF," but what's so likeable about you? Probably a lot more than you think. To find out, first of all, remember that liking *yourself* is the key to being liked by others. Also, recall that you have a racial identity you can be very proud of. Liking yourself doesn't mean copping an attitude. It doesn't mean that you're tripping on anyone else. It just means being cool with the you that's you and refusing to fear the you that's not you. Do you know what you like about you? Let's see.

List the ten things you like BEST about yourself (for example, your sense of humor, your loyalty, your looks).

1. _____

2. _____

3. _____

4. _____

5. _____

6. _____

7. _____

8. _____

9. _____

10. _____

Did you get ten? Did you get more? Way to go!

Feeling Pressured?

WHY MAKE SUCH A BIG DEAL about liking yourself? Well, liking yourself helps you see that your feelings count as much as anyone else's. And liking yourself and knowing that your feelings count as much as anyone else's are your best bets for getting out of the peer pressure cooker. Check out this pressure situation:

A friend offers you a ride home from school on his motorcycle, but you can smell alcohol on his breath.

There are 8 basic ways to escape the heat of peer pressure.

1. **SAY NO**—*No thanks.*

2. **DELAY**—*Not today. Maybe tomorrow.*

3. **LAUGH IT OFF**—*Not unless that hog has training wheels.*

4. **AVOID**—*I can't. I have to go get some stuff from my locker.*

5. **OFFER AN ALTERNATIVE**—*Okay, but I'm doing the driving.*

6. **SPLIT**—*Say no and leave.*

7. **USE PARENTS AS OUTS**—*I can't. My dad would kill me.*

8. **SAY IT THE WAY IT IS**—*No way! You've been drinking.*

Learning to say no to peer pressure takes some practice. Choose one of the following situations. With a partner, use any or all of the seven ways above and practice liking yourself enough to get out of the peer pressure cooker.

Your partner is putting a lot of pressure on you to have sex. You aren't ready for this.

You're at a party with friends. They're all doing cocaine, and they offer you a line.

Your friends want you to come along with them to the record shop where they plan to "lift" a few CDs.

Your Black friends are giving you a lot of heat because you sometimes include your white friends in their group, and they don't like it.

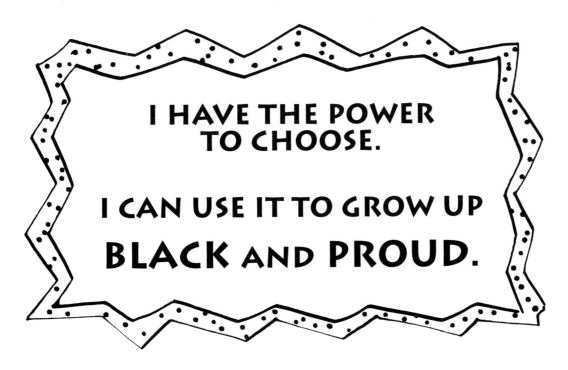

I HAVE THE POWER TO CHOOSE.

I CAN USE IT TO GROW UP BLACK AND PROUD.

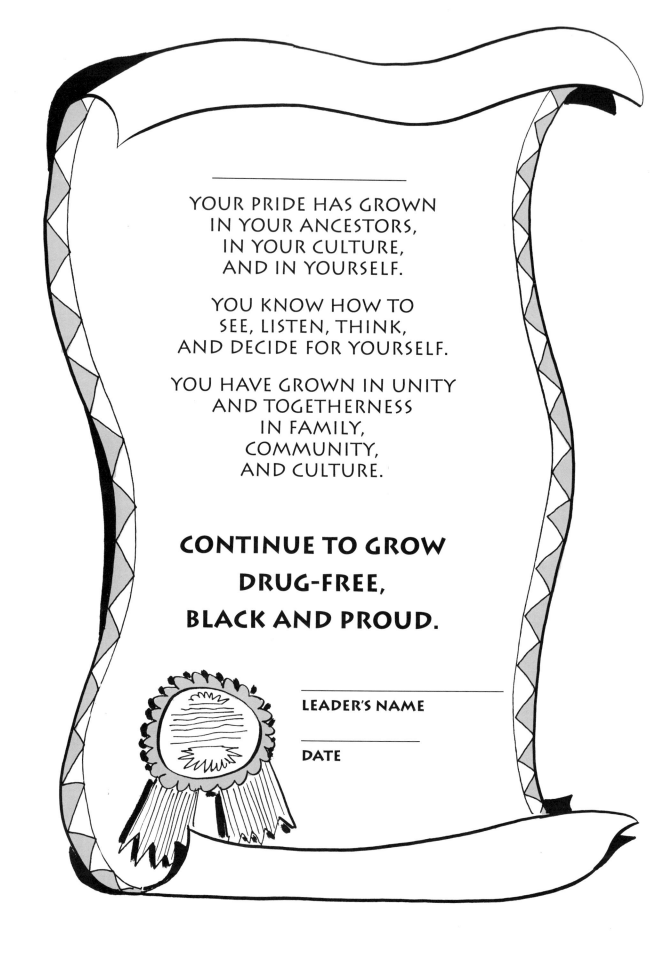

YOUR PRIDE HAS GROWN
IN YOUR ANCESTORS,
IN YOUR CULTURE,
AND IN YOURSELF.

YOU KNOW HOW TO
SEE, LISTEN, THINK,
AND DECIDE FOR YOURSELF.

YOU HAVE GROWN IN UNITY
AND TOGETHERNESS
IN FAMILY,
COMMUNITY,
AND CULTURE.

CONTINUE TO GROW

DRUG-FREE,

BLACK AND PROUD.

LEADER'S NAME

DATE